Pour trouver le divin, il faut d'abord considérer le petit. Les exemples peuvent se trouver parmi les exquises épiphanies visuelles trouvées dans l'art de Michiko Kamee et représentées sur des objets miniatures. Notre couverture Kikka reproduit son dessin « plein de chrysanthèmes » qui fut à l'origine peint à la main avec une glaçure dorée et de couleur sur porcelaine en utilisant le *Kyo-Satsuma*, l'un des grands arts traditionnels de Kyoto.

Michiko Kamee est née en 1978 au Japon, et a fréquenté l'école des arts traditionnels de Kyoto. Après avoir obtenu son diplôme, elle voyagea en Europe et en Asie, en affirmant sa carrière artistique dans les miniatures. Elle concentre la beauté dans ses petites œuvres d'art jusqu'à en faire ressortir la plus pure des extractions. Dans ce modèle, le spectateur peut voir de petites touches kaléidoscopiques de fleurs épanouies, ainsi que le talent artistique simplifié à chaque coup de pinceau et de teinte.

L'interprétation détaillée de Michiko Kamee de l'une des fleurs les plus appréciées montre les techniques de *Kyo-Satsuma*, qui mettent l'accent sur la précision de la ligne et le choix de couleur, accentués par une beauté dorée à vous couper le souffle.

Um das Göttliche zu finden, betrachte das Kleine. Ein gutes Beispiel hierfür sind die erlesenen visuellen Offenbarungen der Künstlerin Michiko Kamee auf Miniaturobjekten. Unser Einband Kikka reproduziert ihr Werk „Voller Chrysanthemen", das ursprünglich auf Porzellan handgemalt und in der Art des *Kyo-Satsuma*, einer traditionellen Handwerkskunst aus Kyoto, mit Goldglasur überzogen war.

Michiko Kamee wurde 1978 in Japan, geboren und studierte an der Kunsthochschule in Kyoto. Nach ihrem Abschluss bereiste sie Europa und Asien und begann ihre künstlerische Karriere der Miniaturmalerei. Sie kondensiert Schönheit auf kleinstem Raum, um ihre reinste Essenz zu erhalten. In diesem Muster lassen sich Spuren eines Kaleidoskops blühender Blumen sowie die exquisite Kunstfertigkeit in jedem Pinselstrich erkennen.

Michiko Kamees detaillierte Wiedergabe einer der am häufigsten dargestellten Blumen ist ein hervorragendes Beispiel von *Kyo-Satsuma* mit höchster Präzision und Farbenfreude, die durch die feine Vergoldung noch betont wird.

Per scoprire le cosa più straordinarie inizia da quelle piccole. Un esempio emblematico sono le deliziose opere di Michiko Kamee, epifanie visuali dipinte su oggetti in miniatura. La copertina Kikka riproduce il motivo "full of chrysanthemum", dipinto a mano su porcellana smaltata policroma con decorazioni in oro *Kyo-Satsuma*, la più conosciuta della tradizione di Kyoto.

Michiko Kamee nasce nel 1978 in Giappone, e frequenta la scuola di arti tradizionali di Kyoto. Terminati gli studi viaggia in Europa e in Asia, definendo la sua carriera artistica nell'ambito delle miniature. Sintetizza tutta la bellezza nelle sue diminute opere d'arte fino a trovare l'essenza più pura. Le pennellate di colore pulite di questo motivo rappresentano caleidoscopio di fiori che sbocciano.

L'opera dettagliata di Michiko Kamee mostra le tecniche *Kyo-Satsuma*, che sottolineano la precisione nella scelta di linee e colore, enfatizzati da una magnifica decorazione in oro.

Para llegar a lo divino hay que detenerse en lo pequeño. Un buen ejemplo son las exquisitas epifanías visuales del arte de Michiko Kamee, que pinta sobre objetos en miniatura. Nuestra cubierta Kikka reproduce su diseño «lleno de crisantemos», pintado a mano sobre porcelana vidriada con motivos policromados y decoraciones en oro mediante *Kyo-Satsuma*, una de las artes tradicionales de Kioto.

Michiko Kamee, que nació en 1978 en Japón, estudió en la Escuela de Artes Tradicionales de Kioto. Al acabar sus estudios viajó por Europa y Asia y enfocó su carrera hacia las miniaturas. Con estas pequeñas obras de arte, la artista busca condensar la belleza hasta obtener su forma más pura. Este diseño es un caleidoscopio de flores en todo su esplendor, y en él se aprecia la delicadeza de cada pincelada y de cada tono.

El nivel de detalle con el que Kamee reproduce estas hermosas flores corresponde a la técnica del *Kyo-Satsuma*, que enfatiza la precisión en las líneas y en los colores, acentuada por una bellísima decoración dorada.

神は細部に宿る。亀江道子の細密画(ミニアチュール)作品には、まさに繊細な神の顕現がいたるところに見られます。本シリーズでは、亀江の「小花詰め」デザインを再現。オリジナル作品は、京薩摩焼の伝統技法を用いながら、陶磁器に色絵金彩で絵付けを施したものとなっています。亀江道子は1978年生まれ。京都伝統工芸専門学校に学び、卒業後はヨーロッパ・アジア各地を旅して細密画の腕を磨きました。亀江は小さな作品の中に美を凝縮していき、美しさはやがて頂点に。「小花詰め」は、花が咲き乱れる万華鏡の華麗なイメージと共に、線と色のひとつひとつに確かな技が感じられるデザインです。

自然の花々を繊密に表現した亀江道子の作品からは、精緻な描線と色使いにこだわる京薩摩焼の技法が見てとれ、息を呑むほどに美しい金彩がアクセントとなっています。

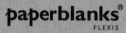

paperblanks®
FLEXIS

Kikka

To find the divine, first consider the small. Case in point are the exquisite visual epiphanies found in Michiko Kamee's art depicted on miniature objects. Our Kikka cover reproduces her "full of chrysanthemum" design originally handpainted with gold overglaze and colour on china by employing *Kyo-Satsuma*, one of the great traditional arts of Kyoto.

Michiko Kamee was born in 1978 in Japan and attended the Traditional Art School of Kyoto. After graduating she travelled throughout Europe and Asia, establishing her artistic career in miniatures. She condenses beauty in her small artworks until it finds its purest distillation. In this design the viewer can see hints of the kaleidoscope of flowers in bloom, as well as fine-boned artistry in every brush stroke and hue.

Michiko Kamee's detailed rendering of one of nature's most celebrated flowers shows off the techniques of *Kyo-Satsuma*, which emphasises precision in line and colour choice, accentuated with breathtakingly beautiful gilding.

ISBN: 978-1-4397-4437-6
ULTRA FORMAT   176 PAGES   LINED
DESIGNED IN CANADA